THE KING AND HIS

Bride

EMBRACING THE BRIDAL
PARADIGM OF THE KINGDOM

TOM CORNELL

THE KING AND HIS BRIDE

EMBRACING THE BRIDAL PARADIGM OF THE
KINGDOM

TOM CORNELL

SOZO PUBLISHING

CONTENTS

Introduction   vii

Part 1: The Song of Solomon   1
1. The King's Unfathomable Love   2
2. The Bride's Insecurity and the King's Assurance   8
3. The Wilderness of Love   14
4. The Bridal Identity   20
   Part 2: The Bridegroom and His Bride   27
5. God as Husband in The Old Testament   28
6. Jesus as the Bridegroom in the New Testament   34
7. The Ten Virgins   40
8. The Apostolic Revelation of the Bride   46
   Part 3: The Marriage Supper of the Lamb   53
9. The Wedding in Heaven   54
10. The New Jerusalem—The Bride Prepared   60
11. The Cry of the Bride and the Spirit   66

Conclusion   73
Appendix A   79
Appendix B   83
Appendix C   85
About the Author   87

INTRODUCTION
THE GREAT INVITATION

A Divine Love Story Written Before Time Began

Before the foundations of the world, a divine romance was set in motion. God was not merely creating a people to serve Him— He was preparing a Bride. The story of Scripture is more than a history of redemption; it is the unfolding of the greatest love story ever told.

From Genesis to Revelation, the Bible reveals a Bridegroom who relentlessly pursues His beloved, longing for the day when they will be united in perfect love. This is not just a theological concept—it is our story. Every believer is invited into this divine romance, called to step beyond the role of a servant and into the identity of the Bride. While many understand their faith through the lens of fatherhood and sonship, few grasp the breathtaking reality that we have also been chosen as a Bride for the King of Kings.

The call of God is not simply to be saved but to be loved—to be fully His. The cross was more than an act of justice; it was a bride price paid in blood. Jesus did not just come to redeem slaves;

He came to win a Bride. At the end of history, when all things reach their fulfillment, we do not see a throne room alone, nor merely a kingdom of servants. We see a wedding—a Bride prepared for her King, standing in radiant glory, ready for eternal union.

Let us be glad and rejoice and give Him glory, for the marriage of the Lamb has come, and His wife has made herself ready." -
Revelation 19:7 NKJV

This book is an invitation to step into the Bridal Paradigm—to see God's love through the lens of marriage, intimacy, and covenant. It is an invitation to leave behind performance-based Christianity and embrace the reality that you are deeply loved, desired, and pursued by the King of the Universe.

The Two Most Intimate Relationships in Scripture

The Bible presents two primary ways in which we relate to God:

1. Father and Son/Daughter – This relationship defines our identity as children of God, heirs of the Kingdom, and recipients of divine inheritance (Romans 8:15-17).
2. Bride and Bridegroom – This relationship defines our intimacy, calling us into covenantal love, voluntary surrender, and eternal partnership (Ephesians 5:25-27).

Both relationships are vital. While sonship establishes our authority and inheritance, the Bridal Paradigm takes us deeper into love, intimacy, and union. Sons inherit the Kingdom, but the Bride reigns beside the King.

Sadly, many believers never step into their bridal identity. They live as servants in the Kingdom, working hard to please God, but they never embrace the reality that they were created to know Him deeply and love Him fully. The question before us is this: Will we merely serve God, or will we become His Bride?

A Love Story from Genesis to Revelation

This divine love story is woven throughout the entire Bible. It is not a minor theme—it is the central storyline of redemption.

In the Beginning: A Garden Wedding

- The first human relationship God established was marriage (Genesis 2:24).
- Adam and Eve's union reflected God's eternal plan— that He would one day have a Bride for Himself.
- The fall of man disrupted this intimacy, but the plan for divine union was never abandoned.

The Old Testament: God as Husband to Israel

- God calls Israel His bride, longing for faithfulness and love (Isaiah 54:5, Jeremiah 3:14).
- Israel's idolatry and rebellion are likened to spiritual adultery (Hosea 2:19-20).
- Yet God never stops pursuing her, demonstrating His relentless, covenantal love.

The Gospels: The Bridegroom Has Come

- John the Baptist calls Jesus the Bridegroom (John 3:29), marking a shift in revelation.
- Jesus teaches about weddings, feasts, and bridal

preparation, pointing to His return for a ready Bride (Matthew 22:1-14, Matthew 25:1-13).
- His first miracle takes place at a wedding (John 2:1-11), symbolizing the greater marriage to come.

The Epistles: The Mystery of Christ and the Church

- Paul reveals that earthly marriage is a prophetic picture of Christ and the Church (Ephesians 5:31-32).
- Believers are described as being betrothed to Christ (2 Corinthians 11:2), awaiting the day of full union.

The Book of Revelation: The Wedding and the Eternal Union

- The final act of history is not a battle or a throne room alone, but a wedding (Revelation 19:7-9).
- The New Jerusalem is described as a Bride adorned for her husband (Revelation 21:2).
- The final cry of the Church is the cry of a longing Bride: The Spirit and the Bride say, "Come!" (Revelation 22:17)

The entire narrative of Scripture points to a King and His Bride, a romance that began before time and will continue for all eternity.

The Call to Intimacy: Why This Matters Now

Understanding the Bridal Paradigm is not just a theological exercise—it transforms the way we live, pray, and pursue Jesus.

- It changes how we see ourselves – We are not just servants trying to please God, but His beloved, invited into deep fellowship.

- It changes how we approach holiness – Instead of striving, we pursue purity out of love, not obligation.
- It changes how we long for Jesus – The return of Christ is no longer a fearful event, but a wedding we eagerly anticipate.

In this book, we will journey through the Song of Solomon, which provides a prophetic roadmap of the Bride's journey—from insecurity and immaturity to full surrender and radiant love. We will also explore how the entire Bible reveals the marriage between Christ and His people, ultimately leading to the Marriage Supper of the Lamb in eternity. At the end of this journey, the hope is that we would not just understand the Bridal Paradigm but embrace it, live it, and long for the Bridegroom with burning love.

The Invitation Is Open—Will You Say Yes?

Jesus is not just a King looking for servants—He is a Bridegroom seeking a Bride. The invitation has been extended. The preparation has begun. The question is: Will we respond? Will we step beyond religious duty and enter into deep, life-altering intimacy? Will we prepare ourselves, clothe ourselves in righteousness, and ready our hearts for His coming? The greatest love story is real. The King is waiting. The Spirit and the Bride say, "Come." Will you say it too?

PART 1: THE SONG OF SOLOMON

THE SONG OF SOLOMON AS THE BLUEPRINT OF THE BRIDES JOURNEY

1

THE KING'S UNFATHOMABLE LOVE

Introduction:
A Love Beyond Human Comprehension.

Love is the most powerful force in the universe. It has driven kings to abandon their thrones, warriors to fight against impossible odds, and lovers to give up everything for the one they cherish. But no earthly romance—no matter how grand—can compare to the love of the King for His Bride.

The Song of Solomon is more than just a poetic love story between Solomon and a Shulamite woman. It is a divinely inspired allegory, revealing the deep, passionate, and relentless love of Christ for His Church. From the beginning of Scripture, we see God pursuing a people for Himself—not as a distant ruler, but as a Bridegroom seeking His beloved.

This love is unfathomable. It defies logic, shatters expectations, and transforms those who dare to receive it. It is the love of a King who chooses a servant girl, woos her, and makes her His own.

In this chapter, we will explore:

- How the Song of Solomon reveals the divine romance between Christ and His Bride.
- The story of the unworthy servant girl and the King's pursuit—a prophetic picture of our journey with Jesus.
- The passionate pursuit of God—how He draws us into love, even when we feel unworthy.

This is the beginning of the Bride's journey—from insecurity and self-doubt to being fully embraced by the King.

1. The Song of Solomon as an Allegory of Christ and the Church

Many approach the Song of Solomon simply as a love poem between Solomon and a woman he loved. But throughout history, scholars and spiritual leaders have recognized it as a prophetic picture of Christ's relationship with His people.

Paul, in Ephesians 5:31-32, reveals that human marriage is a mystery pointing to the greater reality of Christ and His Church: "For this reason a man shall leave his father and mother and be joined to his wife, and the two shall become one flesh. This is a great mystery, but I speak concerning Christ and the church."

If earthly marriage is a reflection of divine love, then the most intimate book in Scripture about love must also point us to Christ and His Bride.

In the Song of Solomon, we see:

- A King who loves a humble bride – a picture of Jesus choosing the Church.
- A Bride who wrestles with her unworthiness – a

picture of our struggle to believe we are truly loved by God.
- A love that deepens through pursuit, separation, and reunion – a picture of the believer's journey toward intimacy with Christ.

The Song of Solomon is not just poetry—it is prophecy. It is a map for the Bride's journey into deeper love.

2. The Servant Girl and the King: The Struggle to Believe We Are Loved

An Unworthy Bride Chosen by a King

The Bride in the Song of Solomon does not begin her journey as a confident queen. She is not a princess from a noble family, nor does she see herself as worthy of royal love. She is a servant girl, tanned from working in the vineyards—an outsider, someone overlooked and rejected by others. She confesses her insecurity immediately:

"I am dark but lovely, O daughters of Jerusalem, Like the tents of Kedar, Like the curtains of Solomon. Do not look upon me, because I am dark, because the sun has tanned me. My mother's sons were angry with me; they made me the keeper of the vineyards, but my own vineyard I have not kept." – Song of Solomon 1:5-6 NKJV

This passage reveals her deep struggles:

- She sees herself as flawed – Her dark skin from working under the sun is a sign that she is a laborer, not royalty.
- She feels unworthy of love – She does not expect a king to desire someone with a past of toil and hardship.

- She has neglected her own soul – While she worked in other people's vineyards, her own vineyard (her own heart) has been left untended.

Many believers live in this place—working hard for God, yet feeling unworthy of intimacy with Him. They labor in ministry, serving the Church, helping others, fulfilling duties, yet they struggle to believe they are truly desired by the King.

God is not looking for perfection—He is looking for love. Though the Bride sees herself as unworthy, the King sees her beauty, her worth, and her destiny.

3. The King's Pursuit: A Love That Transforms

The Bridegroom Speaks: "You Are Beautiful to Me" In response to the Bride's insecurity, the King does not rebuke her or affirm her fears. Instead, He speaks words of love and adoration:

"I have compared you, my love, to my filly among Pharaoh's chariots. Your cheeks are lovely with ornaments, your neck with chains of gold." – Song of Solomon 1:9-10 NKJV

Instead of affirming her flaws, the King declares her beauty. He compares her to Pharaoh's royal horses, known for their strength, grace, and nobility. Though she sees herself as a lowly servant, He sees her as worthy of royal splendor.

The Nature of Divine Pursuit

The King's love is not passive—it is pursuing, relentless, and transformative. The Bride does not chase after the King—He woos her, draws her, and calls her beautiful before she even understands His love.

This mirrors how Jesus pursues His Church:

"We love Him because He first loved us." – 1 John 4:19 NKJV

Before we ever loved God, He loved us. Before we ever pursued intimacy, He was pursuing us. His love is not dependent on our performance—it is rooted in His desire for us as His Bride.

4. The Invitation to Draw Near

The King does not simply speak words of love—He invites the Bride to come closer:

"Rise up, my love, my fair one, and come away." – Song of Solomon 2:10 NKJV

This is the great invitation of divine romance. Jesus does not want a distant, formal relationship with His Church—He wants intimacy, closeness, and shared love.

Yet, many believers struggle to step into intimacy with God. Like the Bride in Song of Solomon, we wrestle with:

- Feelings of unworthiness – "How could God desire someone like me?"
- Fear of intimacy – "What will happen if I fully give my heart to Him?"
- Busyness and distraction – "I don't have time to sit at His feet."

But the King continues to pursue, invite, and call us into deeper love.

Conclusion: Responding to the King's Love

The Bride's journey begins with insecurity and hesitation, but it does not end there. As she encounters the King's love, she will begin to see herself through His eyes. This is our story as well. We often feel unworthy, insecure, and unsure of how to respond to God's love. But the truth is:

- He has already chosen us.
- He has already spoken words of love over us.
- He is already pursuing us.

The only question that remains is: Will we respond? Will we allow His love to transform us? Will we rise up and come away with Him? The King is calling. The Spirit and the Bride say, "Come." Will you answer?

2

THE BRIDE'S INSECURITY AND THE KING'S ASSURANCE

Introduction: Wrestling with Our Worth

Every great love story has moments of doubt—times when the beloved questions, Am I truly worthy of this love? When the King sets His gaze on the Bride, she is overwhelmed—not just by His majesty, but by her own perceived inadequacies. The Song of Solomon captures this tension in the Bride's heart:

> *"I am dark but lovely, O daughters of Jerusalem, Like the tents of Kedar, Like the curtains of Solomon. Do not look upon me, because I am dark, Because the sun has tanned me." – Song of Solomon 1:5-6 NKJV*

Here we find the Bride caught between two realities—her unworthiness ("I am dark") and her beauty in the King's eyes ("but lovely"). This is the same tension many believers experience in their relationship with Jesus. We know that we are flawed, weak, and imperfect, yet... We hear Him call us beautiful, chosen, and beloved.

How do we reconcile this? How can we, as the Bride of

Christ, step beyond shame and insecurity into full intimacy with the King?

In this chapter, we will explore:

1. The struggle of the Bride to see herself as the King sees her.
2. The tension between shame, unworthiness, and the call to intimacy.
3. How the King reassures His Bride, declaring her beautiful despite her insecurities.

This is a transformational moment in the Bride's journey—where she must decide whose voice she will believe: her own insecurities or the words of her Beloved.

1. "I Am Dark But Lovely" – Seeing Ourselves Through the King's Eyes: *The Battle Between Shame and Beauty*

The Bride's first words of self-description reveal a deep internal battle: "I am dark but lovely."

The phrase "I am dark" represents:

- Her awareness of her flaws, sins, and weaknesses.
- Her feelings of unworthiness before the King.
- Her past experiences of rejection and toil.

The phrase "but lovely" reflects:

- A glimmer of hope—Could I really be beautiful in His eyes?
- The tension of knowing God's love is real, but struggling to fully believe it.

This battle still rages in the hearts of believers today.

- We feel the weight of our sin and shortcomings.
- We hesitate to step boldly into intimacy with Jesus.
- We struggle to accept that He truly desires us.

Yet the King sees us through a different lens. The king sees beauty where we see brokenness. Throughout Scripture, we see that God chooses the weak, the unworthy, and the overlooked—not to reject them, but to transform them.

- Moses was insecure about his speech (Exodus 4:10-12), yet God called him to lead a nation.
- Gideon saw himself as the weakest in his family (Judges 6:15), but God called him a mighty warrior.
- Peter denied Jesus three times (Luke 22:61-62), yet Jesus restored him and entrusted him with the Church.

The Bride's insecurity does not disqualify her—it is an opportunity for divine reassurance. The King does not ignore her struggles. He meets her in them.

2. The Struggle Between Shame, Unworthiness, and the Call to Intimacy: *Why Do We Struggle to Believe We Are Loved?*

Many believers live in the tension of knowing God's love in theory but struggling to experience it in reality. Why?

1. We Focus on Our Own Weaknesses Instead of His Love
The Bride's insecurities stem from her past experiences and flaws. She has been:

- Overworked ("They made me keeper of the vineyards" – Song of Solomon 1:6).
- Rejected ("My mother's sons were angry with me").
- Neglected her own heart ("My own vineyard I have not kept").

Many believers fall into this same trap—we are so busy serving God that we neglect personal intimacy with Him. But Jesus did not choose us because of our performance—He chose us because He loves us.

"You did not choose Me, but I chose you." – John 15:16 NKJV

2. We Compare Ourselves to Others

The daughters of Jerusalem represent those who do not struggle with insecurity like the Bride does. She sees herself as less than them. Comparison is one of the greatest enemies of intimacy.

- We look at others and assume they are more worthy of God's love.
- We see their gifts and think we are not enough.
- We hesitate to step into deeper intimacy because we feel unqualified.

But the King does not compare His Bride to others—He sees her as uniquely beautiful.

3. We Listen to the Lies of the Enemy

The enemy has been lying about our worth since the Garden of Eden.

- He told Eve that she was lacking something (Genesis 3:4-5).
- He told Moses that he wasn't qualified (Exodus 4:10).
- He told Joshua the high priest that he was filthy and unworthy (Zechariah 3:1-4).

The same voice whispers to believers today:

- "You are not good enough."
- "You will never be holy enough."
- "You are too broken to be loved."

But Jesus silences every accusation:

"There is therefore now no condemnation for those who are in Christ Jesus." – Romans 8:1 NKJV

The Bride's struggle is not whether she is loved—it is whether she will believe it and step into intimacy.

3. The King's Assurance: Speaking Identity Over His Bride

The King's Response: Declaring Her Beauty In response to the Bride's insecurities, the King does not correct or rebuke her. Instead, He speaks words of love, identity, and affirmation:

"Behold, you are fair, my love! Behold, you are fair! You have dove's eyes." – Song of Solomon 1:15 NKJV

This is a profound moment in their relationship. The Bride says: "I am dark but lovely." The King responds: "You are fair. You are beautiful." Where she sees flaws, He sees radiance. Where she sees unworthiness, He sees a Bride worthy of love.

What It Means to Have "Dove's Eyes"

The King tells the Bride she has dove's eyes. This represents:

- Singleness of vision – A dove has no peripheral vision —it is focused only on one thing.
- Purity and innocence – The eyes are a window to the soul (Matthew 6:22).
- A gaze locked on the King – She is beginning to shift her focus from herself to Him.

This is a turning point in her journey. The more she gazes at Him, the less she will be consumed by her own inadequacies.

Conclusion: Whose Voice Will We Believe?

The Bride's greatest battle is not external—it is internal.

- Will she continue believing her own insecurities?
- Or will she believe the words of the King?

The same question is before us. Jesus has already spoken His love over us.

- He calls us chosen (John 15:16).
- He calls us beautiful (Psalm 45:11).
- He calls us His Bride (Revelation 19:7).

The King is not waiting for us to be perfect before we draw near. He is calling us now. The Spirit and the Bride say, "Come." Will we believe His words? Will we step into intimacy beyond insecurity? The King has spoken. Will we trust His voice?

3

THE WILDERNESS OF LOVE

Introduction: When Love Is Tested

Every great love story faces moments of separation, longing, and pursuit. A love that is never tested remains shallow, but a love that endures trials grows stronger and more unshakable. This is the reality for the Bride in Song of Solomon—after experiencing the King's love, she finds herself in a season where He seems distant, hidden, and absent. In Song of Solomon 3:1-3, the Bride expresses the deep ache of separation:

"By night on my bed I sought the one I love; I sought him, but I did not find him. 'I will rise now,' I said, 'And go about the city; In the streets and in the squares I will seek the one I love.' I sought him, but I did not find him. The watchmen who go about the city found me; I said, 'Have you seen the one I love?'" – Song of Solomon 3:1-3 NKJV

This is a pivotal moment in her journey. She has moved past insecurity and has begun to embrace the King's love, but now He seems distant. The joy of intimacy gives way to longing, and she is forced to seek Him more deeply.

Many believers encounter this same experience in their walk with Christ—seasons where His presence, once so tangible,\ now seems distant. These moments feel like wilderness seasons, where God seems silent, prayers feel unanswered, and the passion that once burned brightly feels like embers barely glowing. But these wilderness seasons are not signs of abandonment—they are seasons of preparation, testing, and deepening love.

In this chapter, we will explore:

- Why the Bridegroom sometimes seems hidden.
- The purpose of testing in love—how God refines us through silence.
- How to respond when we feel distant from God.

At the end of this chapter, we will see that separation is not rejection—it is an invitation to pursue, seek, and hunger for greater depths of intimacy.

1. The Purpose of the Wilderness: *Why Does God Seem to Withdraw?*

Many believers assume that when God feels distant, they must have done something wrong. But in reality, divine hiddenness is often a sign of maturity, not failure. In Song of Solomon 3:1, the Bride searches for the King at night:

"By night on my bed I sought the one I love; I sought him, but I did not find him." – Song of Solomon 3:1 NKJV

She is learning that love is not just about feeling God's presence—it is about seeking Him, even in the dark. Throughout Scripture, God allows seasons of divine silence and testing:

- Abraham waited for the promise of a son for years (Genesis 15:1-6).
- Job endured suffering without explanation, yet declared, "Though He slay me, yet will I trust Him" (Job 13:15).
- Jesus Himself experienced divine silence on the cross, crying out, "My God, My God, why have You forsaken Me?" (Matthew 27:46).

If even Jesus endured a moment of divine silence, then we must recognize that love must sometimes be tested.

The Wilderness Is a Place of Refining

God does not withdraw to punish us—He does so to purify our love.

"I will bring her into the wilderness and speak tenderly to her." –
Hosea 2:14 ESV

The wilderness teaches us to love Jesus for who He is, not just for what He gives.

- When His blessings seem absent, will we still love Him?
- When His voice seems silent, will we still seek Him?
- When our emotions no longer carry us, will we choose to worship?

The true test of love is faithfulness when we feel nothing.

2. Learning Trust and Intimacy in the Secret Place

The Bride's Response: Rising in Pursuit

When the Bride realizes the King is not with her, she does not remain passive. Instead, she rises up to seek Him:

"I will rise now and go about the city; In the streets and in the squares I will seek the one I love." – Song of Solomon 3:2 NKJV

This reveals a crucial principle: when God feels distant, the response should be pursuit, not passivity. Many believers, when faced with spiritual dryness, withdraw.

- They pray less because they don't feel anything.
- They worship less because God doesn't seem near.
- They question His love, assuming something is wrong.

But the Bride teaches us that love does not retreat—it rises. When Jesus seemed asleep in the boat during the storm, the disciples woke Him, saying, "Lord, do You not care that we are perishing?" (Mark 4:38). The truth was, He was always there—but they had to cry out, seek, and wake Him.

The Watchmen and the Seeking Bride

As the Bride searches, she encounters the watchmen—spiritual authorities or leaders:

"The watchmen who go about the city found me; I said, 'Have you seen the one I love?'" – Song of Solomon 3:3 NKJV

In wilderness seasons, God often speaks through others:

- A pastor's sermon may carry the very answer we need.
- A prophetic word may reignite our faith.
- A spiritual mentor may remind us to keep seeking even when we feel dry.

The Bride does not give up—she continues asking, seeking, and knocking.

"Scarcely had I passed them when I found the one I love. I held him and would not let him go." – Song of Solomon 3:4 NKJV

When she finds Him, she clings to Him with new intensity. This is the purpose of the wilderness: it makes us desperate for His presence, unwilling to settle for anything less.

3. The Cry of the Bride: "Have You Seen the One Whom My Soul Loves?"

One of the most profound moments in this passage is the Bride's desperate question:

"Have you seen the one whom my soul loves?" – Song of Solomon 3:3 ESV

This is not just a casual inquiry—it is a lovesick cry. The Mark of a Lovesick Bride When a Bride is in love, she:

1. Seeks relentlessly – She will not rest until she finds Him.
2. Hungers deeply – Nothing else satisfies.
3. Refuses to settle – She does not replace intimacy with ministry, duty, or routine.

This is the same longing that fuels revival, intercession, and the cry of the last-days Church:

"The Spirit and the Bride say, 'Come!'" – Revelation 22:17 NKJV

The cry of the Bride is not just for more blessings—it is for the Bridegroom Himself.

Conclusion: Responding to the Wilderness of Love

The Bride's journey through separation and longing reveals deep truths about our walk with Jesus:

1. Love must be tested to be proven.
2. Seasons of silence are invitations to deeper pursuit.
3. The longing of the Bride fuels greater intimacy.

The wilderness is not punishment—it is preparation. It is where the Bride learns to hunger for the King with all her heart.

- Will we pursue Jesus even when we don't feel Him?
- Will we cry out, "Have you seen the one whom my soul loves?"
- Will we cling to Him with renewed passion when we find Him again?

The Bride's journey is far from over. The King has drawn her deeper into love, and her longing has transformed into a relentless pursuit. The Spirit is stirring the same hunger in His Church today. The Spirit and the Bride say, "Come." Will you answer the call?

THE BRIDAL IDENTITY

Introduction: Becoming Who We Were Always Meant to Be

One of the most profound revelations a believer can receive is the understanding that they are not just saved, not just servants, but the chosen Bride of Christ. This is a transformational shift in identity—from striving to intimacy, from fear to love, from insecurity to confidence. At the beginning of Song of Solomon, the Bride wrestles with feelings of unworthiness:

"I am dark but lovely... Do not look upon me, because I am dark, because the sun has tanned me." – Song of Solomon 1:5-6 NKJV

But by the time she reaches the middle of her journey, something has changed. She declares with boldness and confidence:

"I am my beloved's, and my beloved is mine." – Song of Solomon 6:3 NKJV

This is the moment of revelation—she no longer questions whether she is loved. She knows it. She is no longer a servant girl struggling with insecurity; she is a chosen Bride who belongs to the King.

In this chapter, we will explore:

1. The moment the Bride realizes she is chosen—embracing belonging instead of striving.
2. The process of transformation—how God takes us from servant to the Bride.
3. Learning to see ourselves as Christ sees us—walking in confidence as His Bride.

This is where the Bride stops questioning her place and starts living in the fullness of love.

1. "I Am My Beloved's, and My Beloved Is Mine" – The Revelation of Belonging

From Insecurity to Confidence. When the Bride makes this statement in Song of Solomon 6:3, something is different.

- Before, she felt unworthy.
- Before, she was afraid of rejection.
- Before, she questioned whether the King truly wanted her.

But now, she declares with assurance: "I am my beloved's, and my beloved is mine." This is not just a statement—it is a shift in identity. She has moved from:

- Striving to resting.
- Questioning to knowing.
- Feeling overlooked to walking in confidence.

Many believers live in the constant struggle of trying to earn

God's love, not realizing that they already belong to Him. The moment we realize we are fully loved, fully chosen, and fully His, everything changes.

The Power of Belonging

This shift in identity is the foundation for intimacy.

- A servant works for approval.
- A Bride knows she is already desired.
- A servant tries to earn a place.
- A Bride knows she already has one.

When we realize we belong to Jesus, we no longer:

- Strive for approval—we rest in love.
- Fear rejection—we know we are chosen.
- Compare ourselves to others—we know our identity is secure.

Belonging leads to intimacy. The Bride can now fully receive the King's love because she is no longer doubting her worthiness. This is the same shift Jesus desires for His Church. He is not returning for a hesitant Bride—He is returning for one who knows she is fully His.

2. The Transformation: The Journey From Servant Girl to The Bride

The Bride's transformation throughout Song of Solomon is profound. She starts as a laborer in the vineyards, insecure and unsure, and she ends as a bride, reigning beside the King. This mirrors our journey in Christ.

1. The Servant Girl (Song of Solomon 1:5-6) – Insecure, striving, unsure of love.
2. The Pursued One (Song of Solomon 2:8-14) – Beginning to hear His voice, learning to trust.
3. The Tested One (Song of Solomon 3:1-4) – Searching for Him in the wilderness, growing in desire.
4. The Chosen Bride (Song of Solomon 6:3) – Confident, secure, fully aware of His love.
5. The Reigning Bride (Song of Solomon 8:5-7) – Walking in fullness, set as a seal upon His heart.

This is the process of divine romance—where we move from serving in insecurity to reigning in love.

God's Pattern of Transformation in Scripture

This pattern of transformation is seen throughout Scripture. God always takes ordinary, unqualified people and makes them rulers and brides in His Kingdom.

- Esther was an orphan servant girl, but she became a queen who ruled beside the king (Esther 2:17).
- Joseph was a prisoner, but he was elevated to second-in-command over Egypt (Genesis 41:41-44).
- David was a shepherd boy, but he became the king of Israel (1 Samuel 16:13).

Jesus is not just saving us—He is transforming us. He does not just want servants in His Kingdom—He is preparing a Bride to reign beside Him.

"If we endure, we shall also reign with Him." – 2 Timothy 2:12 NKJV

This is why we must embrace our bridal identity. It is not

arrogance to believe we are chosen—it is humility to receive what He has already declared.

3. Learning to See Ourselves as Christ Sees Us: How Does the King See His Bride?

Throughout Song of Solomon, the King consistently speaks words of beauty, love, and affirmation over the Bride—even when she struggles to believe them.

"You are altogether beautiful, my love; there is no flaw in you." –
Song of Solomon 4:7 ESV

When she sees darkness, He sees radiance. When she feels insecure, He declares her worth. This is how Jesus sees His Church:

- Blameless and spotless (Ephesians 5:27).
- A radiant Bride (Revelation 19:7-8).
- Seated with Him in heavenly places (Ephesians 2:6).

Why We Struggle to See Ourselves Correctly

Many believers struggle to walk in their bridal identity because they still:

1. Define themselves by their past.
2. See their flaws more than God's love.
3. Struggle to accept grace as a gift.

But the King does not define us by our past—He defines us by His love.

- Rahab was a prostitute, but God made her part of Jesus' lineage.

- Peter denied Jesus, but he was restored and became a leader of the Church.
- Paul persecuted Christians, but he was transformed into an apostle.

Jesus is calling us to stop seeing ourselves through the lens of our failures and start seeing ourselves through the lens of His love.

Walking in Bridal Confidence

When the Bride declares "I am my beloved's, and my beloved is mine," she is walking in the confidence of being fully loved. This is what Jesus desires for His Church today:

- A Bride who knows she is loved.
- A Bride who walks in intimacy instead of striving.
- A Bride who is ready for His return.

The question is: Will we step into this identity?

Conclusion: The King Has Already Chosen You

The moment the Bride realizes she is chosen, everything changes. She is no longer striving to be loved—she is resting in love. She is no longer questioning—she is secure. She is no longer unsure—she is confident. This is what Jesus desires for His Church. He is not returning for a hesitant Bride—He is returning for a Bride who knows she is fully His. The Spirit and the Bride say, "Come." Will you step into your bridal identity today?

PART 2: THE BRIDEGROOM AND HIS BRIDE

THE BRIDEGROOM AND HIS BRIDE THROUGHOUT SCRIPTURE

5

GOD AS HUSBAND IN THE OLD TESTAMENT

Introduction: A Love Story Written in Covenant

From the beginning, God's relationship with His people has been marked by covenant love. While many view the Old Testament primarily through the lens of law and judgment, beneath the surface lies a divine romance—the story of a faithful God pursuing an unfaithful bride. This theme of God as Husband is woven throughout the Old Testament.

He does not just call Israel His people; He calls them His Bride. He is not just a King or a Judge—He is a passionate Lover who desires intimacy with His chosen ones. Yet, the tragedy of Israel's history is that they repeatedly turned away from their Husband, breaking covenant through idolatry, rebellion, and spiritual adultery. But even in their unfaithfulness, God's love never failed. His longing for restoration and intimacy remained unshaken, pointing to a future fulfillment in Christ and His Church.

In this chapter, we will explore:

1. Israel as God's unfaithful but beloved Bride (Isaiah 54:5, Jeremiah 3:14).
2. The prophetic imagery of Hosea—God's relentless love for His wayward people.
3. The bridal calling of Israel and its fulfillment in the Church.

Through this, we will see that God's desire for a Bride did not begin in the New Testament—it was always His plan.

1. Israel as God's Unfaithful but Beloved Bride

God Declares Himself as Israel's Husband

One of the clearest revelations of God as Husband is found in the book of Isaiah:

"For your Maker is your husband, the Lord of hosts is His name; And your Redeemer is the Holy One of Israel; He is called the God of the whole earth." – Isaiah 54:5 NKJV

This is not just a metaphor—it is a declaration of divine covenant.

- God did not simply choose Israel as a nation—He married her.
- The covenant between God and Israel was not just a legal agreement—it was a sacred marriage vow.
- Israel was not just a servant of God—she was His Bride, chosen to be set apart for Him alone.

Yet, despite this covenantal love, Israel struggled with faithfulness.

Israel's Repeated Unfaithfulness

Throughout the Old Testament, Israel's relationship with God follows a tragic cycle:

1. God pursues and blesses Israel (Deuteronomy 7:6-9).
2. Israel turns to idols and foreign gods (Judges 2:11-13).
3. God warns them of judgment and calls them back (Jeremiah 2:2-3).
4. Israel repents and returns—for a time.
5. The cycle repeats.

This is why God speaks with the language of heartbreak in Jeremiah 3:14:

"Return, O backsliding children," says the Lord; "for I am married to you." – Jeremiah 3:14 NKJV

God is not just disappointed—He is a betrayed Husband, pleading for His Bride to return. This pattern ultimately foreshadows the need for a new covenant—one that will not be based on Israel's faithfulness, but on the faithfulness of the Bridegroom Himself.

2. The Prophetic Imagery of Hosea—God's Relentless Love

One of the most dramatic pictures of God's love in the Old Testament is found in the book of Hosea. God commands the prophet Hosea to marry a prostitute named Gomer—a woman who repeatedly betrays him, abandons him, and sells herself to other lovers. Yet, despite her unfaithfulness, Hosea continues to pursue her, redeem her, and love her.

A Prophetic Parable of God's Love

This shocking story is not just about Hosea and Gomer—it is a prophetic parable of God and Israel.

"Then the Lord said to me, 'Go again, love a woman who is loved by a lover and is committing adultery, just like the love of the Lord for the children of Israel, who look to other gods.'" - Hosea 3:1 NKJV

Hosea represents God. Gomer represents Israel (and humanity as a whole). Despite Israel's spiritual adultery, God does not abandon His Bride. Instead, He pursues, redeems, and restores.

God's Promise of Restoration

Even in His judgment, God promises to one day restore His Bride:

"I will betroth you to Me forever; Yes, I will betroth you to Me in righteousness and justice, in lovingkindness and mercy." - Hosea 2:19 NKJV

This is a prophetic glimpse of the coming of Jesus Christ— the Bridegroom who will redeem His Bride not with silver or gold, but with His own blood (1 Peter 1:18-19).

3. The Bridal Calling of Israel and Its Fulfillment in the Church

The Promise of a New Covenant

Because of Israel's repeated spiritual adultery, a new covenant was necessary. Jeremiah prophesied:

"Behold, the days are coming, says the Lord, when I will make a new covenant with the house of Israel." - Jeremiah 31:31 NKJV

This covenant would be:

- Written on hearts instead of stone (Jeremiah 31:33).
- Established through the faithfulness of the Bridegroom (Jesus), rather than the unfaithfulness of the Bride.
- Extended beyond Israel—to include the Gentiles, forming one new Bride.

The Bride Expands—The Gentiles Are Brought In

In the Old Testament, God's Bride was Israel. But through Jesus, the invitation extends to all nations. Paul explains:

"You who were once far off have been brought near by the blood of Christ." - Ephesians 2:13 NKJV

Now, both Jews and Gentiles are part of one Bride, united under the new covenant of Christ's love. This is why the New Testament Church is called the Bride of Christ (Ephesians 5:25-27, Revelation 19:7).

Conclusion: A Love That Never Gives Up

The Old Testament reveals that God's desire for a Bride was always part of His plan.

- He pursued Israel as His Bride.
- Even in her unfaithfulness, He never stopped loving her.
- He sent prophets to call her back, and He promised a new covenant where faithfulness would be sealed by the Bridegroom Himself.

This is the love story of redemption.

- It is not about our ability to remain faithful—it is about God's relentless pursuit.
- It is not about what we do to earn His love—it is about the love that has already been given.
- It is not just about Israel—it is about the Church, the redeemed Bride of Christ, who is being prepared for the Marriage Supper of the Lamb.

The Spirit and the Bride say, "Come." Will we respond to this divine invitation to intimacy and covenant love?

JESUS AS THE BRIDEGROOM IN THE NEW TESTAMENT

Introduction: The Arrival of the Bridegroom

For centuries, Israel awaited the fulfillment of God's covenant promises—the day when He would fully restore His people and establish an unbreakable union with them. Throughout the Old Testament, God's relationship with Israel was often described in marital terms, but there was always a longing for a deeper, final fulfillment.

When Jesus stepped onto the scene, He did not merely come as a teacher, a prophet, or a king—He came as the long-awaited Bridegroom. His mission was not just to establish a Kingdom, but to call and prepare a Bride. From the beginning of His ministry, Jesus revealed Himself as the Bridegroom:

- John the Baptist recognized Him as such (John 3:29).
- His first miracle at a wedding pointed to a greater wedding to come (John 2:1-11).
- His parables repeatedly used wedding imagery to describe the Kingdom (Matthew 22, Luke 14).

In this chapter, we will explore how Jesus unveiled His role as the divine Bridegroom, fulfilling the long-awaited marriage covenant between God and His people.

1. John the Baptist's Declaration: The Friend of the Bridegroom

John's Prophetic Announcement

John the Baptist was the last and greatest prophet under the Old Covenant. His role was to prepare the way for the Messiah, and when Jesus arrived, John did not hesitate to identify Him not just as the Lamb of God, but as the Bridegroom. John declared:

> *"He who has the bride is the bridegroom; but the friend of the bridegroom, who stands and hears him, rejoices greatly because of the bridegroom's voice. Therefore, this joy of mine is fulfilled." –*
> *John 3:29 NKJV*

This statement is profound for several reasons:

- John identifies Jesus as the Bridegroom – He is not merely a teacher or a prophet; He has come for a Bride.
- John calls himself the "friend of the Bridegroom" – This echoes the role of a Jewish wedding attendant (Shoshben), who was responsible for ensuring that the Bride was prepared for her wedding.
- John's joy is complete because the Bridegroom has arrived – His mission was not to build his own following but to point the Bride to Jesus.

The Transition from the Old Covenant to the New John's declaration signals a major shift in redemptive history:

- The Old Covenant prepared the way, but now the Bridegroom had come to establish a new and greater covenant.
- The law and the prophets pointed to God's love for His people, but now that love would be fully revealed in Christ's pursuit of His Bride.
- The wilderness of longing was ending, and the joy of union was beginning.

This is why John's disciples struggled to understand the shift. When they noticed that Jesus' followers were growing, they questioned John. But John's response was clear:

"He must increase, but I must decrease." – John 3:30 NKJV

The Bride belongs to Jesus, not to any other leader. John's role was to prepare the way for the wedding—Jesus came to fulfill it.

2. The Wedding at Cana: A Prophetic Sign of the Coming Marriage

Jesus' First Miracle Takes Place at a Wedding

One of the most intriguing aspects of Jesus' ministry is that His first miracle was not performed in a temple, a synagogue, or before religious leaders—it was at a wedding.

"On the third day there was a wedding in Cana of Galilee, and the mother of Jesus was there. Now both Jesus and His disciples were invited to the wedding." – John 2:1-2 NKJV

When the wine ran out, Jesus turned water into wine, marking the beginning of His public ministry (John 2:3-11).

The Symbolism of Cana and the Coming Wedding Feast

This was not just a random setting—this was a prophetic sign.

1. The Bridegroom Provides the Wine

- In Jewish culture, it was the responsibility of the bridegroom to provide wine for the wedding feast.
- When the wine ran out, it was a picture of the limitations of the Old Covenant—the old wine had run dry, and a new covenant was needed.
- Jesus, as the true Bridegroom, provided the best wine, signifying that He was ushering in something greater.

2. The Third Day Symbolism

- The wedding took place on the third day (John 2:1), pointing to Jesus' resurrection on the third day—the ultimate moment of victory for His Bride.

3. The Best Wine for the End

- The master of the feast was astonished, saying: "You have kept the good wine until now!" (John 2:10)
- This is a picture of the final wedding feast—the Marriage Supper of the Lamb—where the best wine (the fullness of intimacy with Christ) will be revealed (Revelation 19:7-9).

Jesus' first miracle was not just about meeting a need—it was a prophetic statement. He had come as the Bridegroom to bring the new wine of the Kingdom.

3. Jesus' Parables of the Wedding Feast

Throughout His ministry, Jesus repeatedly used wedding imagery to describe the Kingdom of Heaven. The Parable of the Wedding Feast (Matthew 22:1-14) In this parable, a king prepares a wedding banquet for his son, but those invited refuse to come. In response, the king invites others—both good and bad—to fill the wedding hall. Key Themes:

1. The Father is preparing a wedding for the Son – The entire purpose of history is moving toward a wedding between Jesus and His Bride.
2. The invited guests rejected the invitation – Many who were originally chosen (Israel's leaders) rejected the Messiah, so the invitation was extended to all nations (Gentiles included).
3. A wedding garment is required – One guest tries to enter without the proper garment, representing those who try to enter the Kingdom without the righteousness of Christ.

"For many are called, but few are chosen." (Matthew 22:14) Only those clothed in Christ's righteousness will be ready for the wedding. The Parable of the Great Banquet (Luke 14:16-24) In this parable, a man invites guests to a great banquet, but they make excuses and refuse to come. The master then invites the poor, the crippled, the blind, and the lame to fill his house. Key Themes:

- Many reject the invitation – Excuses keep people from intimacy with Jesus.
- The invitation extends to the outcasts – The Bride is made up of those who recognize their need for the Bridegroom.
- There is a sense of urgency – The Master says,

"Compel them to come in, so that my house may be full" (Luke 14:23).

This parable reveals the heart of Jesus as the Bridegroom—He desires a full wedding feast.

Conclusion: The Bridegroom Is Calling—Will We Respond?

Jesus did not just come to teach, heal, or perform miracles—He came as the Bridegroom, seeking a Bride.

- John the Baptist recognized Him as the Bridegroom.
- His first miracle at a wedding foreshadowed the greater wedding to come.
- His parables reveal that the invitation to the wedding feast is open—but not all will accept.

The Spirit and the Bride say, "Come." Will we accept the invitation? Will we prepare for the coming wedding? The King is preparing a wedding feast in heaven. Will we be found ready?

THE TEN VIRGINS

THE BRIDESMAIDS IN THE KINGDOM

Introduction: A Bride in Waiting

Every wedding has a waiting period. The Bride does not meet her Groom at the altar without first preparing herself. In ancient Jewish culture, once a bride was betrothed, she entered a season of preparation, not knowing the exact day or hour her bridegroom would return to take her to the wedding feast. This is the season the Church is in now—we are the Betrothed Bride of Christ, waiting for our Bridegroom's return.

But Jesus warned us that not everyone who is waiting will be ready. Some will be wise, prepared, and full of oil, while others will be foolish, unprepared, and left outside the wedding feast. In one of His most sobering parables, Jesus describes the Ten Virgins —ten bridesmaids awaiting the arrival of the Bridegroom. The difference between them was oil—the fuel that sustained their lamps as they waited through the night.

In this chapter, we will explore:

1. The waiting period of the Bride before the Bridegroom's return—understanding the Jewish wedding tradition and its prophetic significance.
2. The oil of intimacy—the difference between the wise and foolish virgins.
3. The call to readiness for the Marriage Supper of the Lamb—why preparation is urgent.

At the end of this chapter, we will see that the greatest tragedy is not rejection by the Bridegroom, but failing to prepare for Him.

1. The Waiting Period: The Bride's Season of Preparation

The Jewish Wedding and the Unknown Hour

In ancient Jewish weddings, once a betrothal (engagement) was made, the bride and groom were considered legally married, but they did not yet live together. Instead, the groom would leave to prepare a place for his bride, and the bride would remain watching, waiting, and preparing herself.

The groom's return for his bride was a joyful surprise. He would come at an unexpected hour, often in the night, accompanied by a loud shout and the sound of a trumpet blast. This tradition is exactly what Jesus referenced in John 14:2-3:

"I go to prepare a place for you. And if I go and prepare a place for you, I will come again and receive you to Myself; that where I am, there you may be also." – John 14:2-3 NKJV

We, as the Bride of Christ, are in this season of waiting—betrothed but not yet fully united, longing for the moment our Bridegroom returns to take us to the wedding feast. Jesus warned us that some will be ready for His return and some will not.

2. The Oil of Intimacy: The Wise and Foolish Virgins The Parable of the Ten Virgins

"Then the kingdom of heaven shall be likened to ten virgins who took their lamps and went out to meet the bridegroom. Now five of them were wise, and five were foolish." – Matthew 25:1-2 NKJV

In this parable:

- All ten were virgins—they were set apart for the wedding.
- All ten had lamps—they had light and expectation.
- All ten were waiting for the Bridegroom—they had the right focus.

But only five were ready.

"The foolish ones took their lamps but did not take any oil with them. The wise ones, however, took oil in jars along with their lamps." – Matthew 25:3-4 NIV

The wise virgins brought extra oil, but the foolish virgins did not. When the Bridegroom came at midnight, the foolish virgins' lamps were going out, and they realized too late that they had no oil. This parable reveals one of the most sobering truths about the Church:

- There will be many who claim to be waiting for Jesus but will not be ready when He comes.
- There will be those who assume their past devotion is enough, but will find themselves empty when the time arrives.
- There will be a cry at midnight, and only those prepared will enter the feast.

What Does the Oil Represent?

The oil in this parable is symbolic of what sustains us in the waiting. It represents:

- Intimacy with Jesus – A real, daily relationship with the Bridegroom.
- The Holy Spirit – The anointing that fuels our spiritual life (Zechariah 4:6).
- Personal Preparation – A life cultivated in prayer, fasting, obedience, and devotion.

The foolish virgins assumed that their initial flame was enough, but they did not maintain their oil supply. This is a warning to believers who rely on past experiences rather than ongoing intimacy.

- Oil cannot be borrowed – The wise virgins could not give their oil to the foolish ones. Intimacy with God is not transferable.
- The door was shut – When the Bridegroom came, those who were unprepared were locked outside.

"Afterward the other virgins came also, saying, 'Lord, Lord, open to us!' But He answered and said, 'Assuredly, I say to you, I do not know you.'" – Matthew 25:11-12 NKJV

The greatest tragedy is not just being left out of the wedding feast—but hearing Jesus say, "I do not know you." This reveals that the oil represents more than just being ready for His return—it represents true relationship with Him.

3. The Call to Readiness for the Marriage Supper of the Lamb Readiness Is Urgent

Jesus concluded the parable with a clear warning:

"Watch therefore, for you know neither the day nor the hour in which the Son of Man is coming." – Matthew 25:13 NKJV

Many put off preparation, assuming there will always be time later. But the reality is:

- The cry at midnight is sudden.
- The door will be shut.
- Not everyone who claims to know Jesus will be welcomed in.

The Marriage Supper of the Lamb is a real event that will take place at the culmination of history. Only those who are ready will sit at the table.

"Let us rejoice and be glad and give Him glory! For the wedding of the Lamb has come, and His Bride has made herself ready." – Revelation 19:7 NIV

This means our preparation is our responsibility.

How Do We Stay Ready?

1. Keep our lamps burning – Stay filled with prayer, worship, and hunger for God (Luke 12:35).
2. Store up oil daily – Build a lifestyle of intimacy with Jesus, not just moments of passion.
3. Stay watchful and expectant – Live every day as though Jesus could return at any moment (Matthew 24:42).
4. Walk in obedience and holiness – The Bride must make herself ready through righteousness (Revelation 19:8).

The Spirit is calling the Church to prepare, but the question is: Will we respond before the door is shut?

Conclusion: Will We Be Wise or Foolish?

This parable is not about unbelievers—it is about the Church. It is about those who claim to be waiting for Jesus but will not all be ready when He comes.

- Five were wise—they lived for intimacy and preparation.
- Five were foolish—they assumed they were ready but were not.
- All were waiting—but not all entered the feast.

Jesus is returning for a Bride who is watching, waiting, and burning with love for Him. The Spirit and the Bride say, "Come." Will we be found ready? Or will we realize too late that we have no oil?

THE APOSTOLIC REVELATION OF THE BRIDE

Introduction: The Mystery of Christ and the Church

Throughout history, God's desire for a Bride has remained the central theme of redemption. From the covenant with Israel to the arrival of the Bridegroom in Jesus, the love story has unfolded step by step. But in the New Testament, the apostolic revelation of the Bride is fully unveiled—declaring that this divine romance was always pointing to something greater. The Apostle Paul, through divine revelation, unveils the mystery hidden for ages:

"For this reason a man shall leave his father and mother and be joined to his wife, and the two shall become one flesh. This mystery is great, but I am speaking of Christ and the Church." – Ephesians 5:31-32 NKJV

Paul declares that earthly marriage is merely a shadow of a greater reality—the union between Jesus and His Bride, the Church. This is not just poetic imagery; it is the ultimate purpose of redemption.

In this chapter, we will explore:

1. Paul's teaching on the Bride of Christ—the mystery of divine union.
2. The betrothal and preparation process in the early Church—what it means to be engaged to Christ.
3. The final cry of the Bride in intercession—the Spirit and the Bride say, "Come" (Revelation 22:17).

The Apostolic revelation is that we are not just believers, disciples, or servants—we are the Bride being made ready for the King.

1. Paul's Teaching: "This Mystery Is Great"

Marriage as a Prophetic Picture

When Paul speaks about marriage in Ephesians 5, he is not simply giving advice for husbands and wives. He is unveiling one of the deepest mysteries of Scripture—that human marriage is a reflection of Christ's relationship with the Church.

"Husbands, love your wives, just as Christ also loved the Church and gave Himself up for her." – Ephesians 5:25 NKJV

In this passage, Paul teaches that:

- Jesus is the Bridegroom, and the Church is His Bride.
- The love between a husband and wife is a prophetic sign of the divine romance.
- The sacrifice of Christ on the cross was the ultimate bride price—the cost He paid to purchase His beloved.

Then, Paul makes the profound statement:

"This mystery is great, but I am speaking of Christ and the Church." – Ephesians 5:32 NKJV

This means that from the very beginning:

- Marriage was always meant to point to something greater.
- Every covenant God made was a foreshadowing of the eternal union between Jesus and His people.
- The end of history is not just about a kingdom—it is about a wedding.

Jesus did not come just to rule a people—He came to win a Bride.

Cleansing and Preparing the Bride

Paul goes further, explaining that Christ's goal is to prepare His Bride in purity and glory:

"That He might sanctify and cleanse her with the washing of water by the word, that He might present her to Himself a glorious Church, not having spot or wrinkle or any such thing, but that she should be holy and without blemish." – Ephesians 5:26-27 NKJV

This means:

1. We are currently in the preparation process.
2. Jesus is actively cleansing, refining, and purifying His Bride.
3. The Bride must be made ready before the wedding feast.

The call to holiness is not legalism—it is bridal preparation. Just as a bride purifies herself for her wedding day, the Church must make herself ready for the return of the Bridegroom (Revelation 19:7).

2. The Betrothal and Preparation Process in the Early Church

The Jewish Betrothal Custom

In Jewish culture, marriage had two phases:

- Betrothal (Engagement) – The couple was legally married but did not yet live together.
- The Wedding Ceremony – The groom would return unexpectedly to take his bride home.

This mirrors our current position as the Bride of Christ:

- We are betrothed to Jesus (2 Corinthians 11:2).
- He has gone to prepare a place for us (John 14:2).
- We are waiting for His return at an unknown hour (Matthew 25:1-13).

The early Church lived with this expectation—that Jesus, the Bridegroom, could return at any moment. This is why Paul describes believers as those who are watching, waiting, and longing for His appearing (Titus 2:13).

The Bride Must Make Herself Ready

John's vision in Revelation confirms that the wedding will not take place until the Bride is prepared:

"The marriage of the Lamb has come, and His Bride has made herself ready." – Revelation 19:7 NKJV

This tells us that:

- The Bride has a role in preparing herself.

- Jesus is returning for a Bride who is fully devoted, mature, and ready for union.
- Not everyone in the Church will be found prepared.

The preparation process involves:

- Intimacy with Jesus – Growing in love, prayer, and devotion.
- Holiness and purity – Removing anything that competes with love for Him.
- Spiritual maturity – Becoming a Bride who can reign with Him.

Many believers see themselves as servants, but the true calling is bridal partnership—ruling and reigning with Jesus as His co-heirs (Romans 8:17).

3. The Bridal Intercession: The Spirit and the Bride Say, "Come" The Final Cry of the Bride

At the end of Scripture, in the final chapter of Revelation, we hear the last recorded prayer in the Bible:

"The Spirit and the Bride say, 'Come!' And let him who hears say, 'Come!'" – Revelation 22:17 NKJV

This is not a casual prayer—this is the deepest cry of love and longing. The Bride does not just desire revival, blessing, or a move of God—she desires the return of the Bridegroom Himself.

The Spirit and the Bride in Agreement

The Holy Spirit's role in the last days is to awaken the Bride's longing for Jesus. When we are filled with the Spirit, our hearts begin to cry out:

"Come, Lord Jesus." – Revelation 22:20 NKJV

This is the mark of a mature Bride—she longs for union more than anything else.

- She is not distracted by worldly pleasures.
- She is not fearful of His return.
- She is ready and eagerly expecting Him.

Jesus is returning for a Bride who is crying out for Him.

Conclusion: Will We Answer the Bridal Call?

The apostolic revelation of the Bride is clear:

1. Jesus is the Bridegroom, and we are His Bride.
2. We are currently in the betrothal season, preparing for His return.
3. Only those who are ready will enter the wedding feast.

The question before us is: Will we live as those preparing for the greatest wedding in history? Will we make ourselves ready? Will we cultivate oil in intimacy? Will we join the cry of the Spirit and the Bride: "Come"? The invitation stands. The Spirit is calling. The Bride must answer.

PART 3: THE MARRIAGE SUPPER OF THE LAMB

THE FINAL CONSUMMATION—THE MARRIAGE SUPPER OF THE LAMB

9

THE WEDDING IN HEAVEN

I ntroduction: The Culmination of All Things

Every love story has a climax, a moment when longing is fulfilled, and promises are realized. From the foundation of the world, God has been preparing a wedding—the union of His Son, Jesus, with His Bride, the Church.

The Bible begins with a marriage in Eden (Genesis 2:24) and ends with a marriage in heaven (Revelation 19:7-9). The entire arc of Scripture leads to this final moment—the Marriage Supper of the Lamb. John, caught up in heavenly vision, records the greatest celebration in history: "Let us rejoice and be glad and give Him glory! For the wedding of the Lamb has come, and His Bride has made herself ready. Fine linen, bright and clean, was given her to wear."

Then the angel said to me, "Write this: Blessed are those who are invited to the wedding supper of the Lamb!" And he added, "These are the true words of God." (Revelation 19:7-9) This is the fulfillment of every longing, every prophecy, and every divine promise. The King has come for His Bride. The waiting is over.

In this chapter, we will explore:

1. Revelation 19:7-9—The culmination of history in the wedding feast.
2. The Bridal Garment—Righteous acts of the saints.
3. The invitation to every believer to take their place at the feast.

This moment is the reason Jesus came, suffered, and redeemed a people—not just to save them, but to marry them, dwell with them, and reign with them forever.

1. Revelation 19:7-9—The Marriage Supper of the Lamb

The Heavenly Celebration Begins

The vision John sees in Revelation 19 is a heavenly wedding celebration like no other. The Bride has been prepared, the feast is set, and all of heaven erupts in praise. "Let us rejoice and be glad and give Him glory! For the wedding of the Lamb has come, and His Bride has made herself ready." (Revelation 19:7)

At this moment:

- The longing of the Bride is fulfilled.
- The waiting Church is united with Jesus.
- The celebration of eternity begins.

This is not a small event—it is the climax of redemptive history. Every covenant, prophecy, and promise leads to this final wedding feast. Jesus Himself foreshadowed this moment when He spoke to His disciples at the Last Supper:

"I tell you, I will not drink from this fruit of the vine from now on

until that day when I drink it new with you in My Father's kingdom." – Matthew 26:29 NKJV

The Bridegroom has been waiting. At this wedding feast, He will drink with His Bride again.

2. The Bridal Garment—Righteous Acts of the Saints

The Bride's Attire: A Garment of Righteousness

John describes the clothing of the Bride: "Fine linen, bright and clean, was given her to wear." (Revelation 19:8) He then explains what this linen represents: "Fine linen stands for the righteous acts of the saints." This tells us that our preparation for the wedding feast is not passive—the Bride is clothed in righteousness, holiness, and purity.

What Does This Garment Represent?

1. The Righteousness of Christ – First and foremost, the Bride's beauty comes from the righteousness given to her through Jesus' sacrifice (2 Corinthians 5:21).
2. Faithful Obedience and Devotion – The Bride is clothed in her acts of love, purity, and faithfulness—not as a way to earn salvation, but as an expression of her love for the Bridegroom.
3. The Beauty of a Prepared Bride – Just as an earthly bride prepares her wedding gown with care, the Church must prepare herself for the return of Jesus.

The spotless Bride of Revelation 19 is the fulfillment of Ephesians 5:27, where Paul describes Jesus' goal: "That He might present her to Himself as a glorious Church, without stain or wrinkle or any such blemish, but holy and blameless." This means:

- Not every believer will be equally prepared.
- Some will have invested in intimacy and purity, while others neglected their preparation.
- The Marriage Supper is for those who have made themselves ready.

The greatest tragedy would be to stand before the King unprepared for the wedding.

3. The Invitation to the Wedding Feast

"Blessed Are Those Who Are Invited"

After describing the wedding, the angel gives a final declaration: "Blessed are those who are invited to the wedding supper of the Lamb!" (Revelation 19:9) This statement reveals something profound:

- Not everyone will enter this wedding feast.
- Many are invited, but not all will accept.
- The door will one day be shut.

This echoes Jesus' parables about the wedding feast (Matthew 22:1-14, Matthew 25:1-13), where:

- Some were invited but refused to come.
- Some tried to enter without proper garments.
- Some were wise and prepared, while others were left outside.

The Marriage Supper of the Lamb is not automatic—it is for those who have accepted the invitation and made themselves ready.

4. The Tragic Reality: Some Will Miss the Wedding

The Foolish Virgins Are Shut Out

In Matthew 25, Jesus tells the Parable of the Ten Virgins. The wise virgins had oil and were ready, but the foolish virgins were unprepared. When the Bridegroom came, the foolish virgins tried to enter but found the door shut:

"Later the others also came. 'Lord, Lord,' they said, 'open the door for us!' But He replied, 'Truly I tell you, I do not know you.'" –
Matthew 25:11-12 NIV

This is the greatest tragedy in eternity—to believe you are part of the wedding, only to hear the Bridegroom say, "I do not know you." The question is not whether Jesus loves us—He already paid the highest price. The question is: Will we prepare for the wedding?

Conclusion: The Spirit and the Bride Say, "Come"

At the very end of the Bible, after the vision of the wedding, the final words of Scripture are an invitation:

"The Spirit and the Bride say, 'Come!' And let him who hears say, 'Come!'" – Revelation 22:17 NKJV

This is the cry of the prepared Bride—not just for revival, not just for a move of God, but for the return of the Bridegroom. The question is:

- Are we preparing for the wedding?
- Are we storing up oil, walking in holiness, and longing for Jesus?
- Are we living as those who know the wedding is near?

The Bridegroom is coming. The feast is being prepared. The invitations have been sent. The Spirit is calling. The Bride must answer. Will we be ready when He comes?

THE NEW JERUSALEM—THE BRIDE PREPARED

I ntroduction: The Final Fulfillment of the Bridal Paradigm

From the first moment of creation, God's desire has been to dwell with His people. Throughout history, He has pursued intimacy with humanity—not as a distant ruler, but as a Bridegroom longing for His Bride.

In the Old Testament, God's presence dwelt in a temple made of stone. In the New Testament, His presence was revealed through Jesus, the Bridegroom in human flesh. But in eternity, God's presence will permanently dwell with His people in the most intimate way imaginable—in a city that is not just a location, but a prepared Bride. John, in his final vision, sees this reality unfolding:

"I saw the Holy City, the new Jerusalem, coming down out of heaven from God, prepared as a bride beautifully dressed for her husband. And I heard a loud voice from the throne saying, 'Behold, the dwelling place of God is now among His people, and He will dwell with them. They will be His people, and God

Himself will be with them and be their God.'" – Revelation 21:2-3 NIV

This is the climax of history—the moment when the Bride and the Bridegroom are finally united forever. The separation caused by sin is gone. The longing of the Bride is fulfilled. The earthly waiting is over, and eternal union begins.

In this chapter, we will explore:

1. Revelation 21:2-3—The Holy City as the adorned Bride.
2. The eternal dwelling of God with His people.
3. Living as the Bride in eternity—what it means to reign and dwell with Christ forever.

This is our eternal destiny—not just to be saved, but to live in union with Jesus for all eternity.

1. The New Jerusalem—The Holy City as the Adorned Bride

A City That Is Also a Bride

John's vision in Revelation is both surprising and glorious. He sees a city descending from heaven, but this is no ordinary city —it is the Bride of Christ, prepared for her husband (Revelation 21:2). This tells us something profound:

- The New Jerusalem is not just a physical place—it is a people.
- The city is the Bride—meaning we, the redeemed Church, are the dwelling place of God.
- The wedding is not just an event—it is an eternal reality.

A City of Radiance and Glory

John describes the New Jerusalem as shining with the glory of God:

"It shone with the glory of God, and its brilliance was like that of a very precious jewel, like jasper, clear as crystal." – Revelation 21:11 NIV

This is the fulfillment of Jesus' words in Matthew 5:14: "You are the light of the world. A city set on a hill cannot be hidden." The Bride—now fully perfected—shines with the radiant light of the glory of God. Every trace of sin, brokenness, and imperfection has been removed. The Bride is completely transformed into the image of Christ (2 Corinthians 3:18). This is our eternal destiny—to be one with Him in perfect love and holiness.

2. The Eternal Dwelling of God with His People

God's Ultimate Desire Fulfilled

One of the most powerful statements can be found in Revelation 21:3:

"Behold, the dwelling place of God is now among His people, and He will dwell with them. They will be His people, and God Himself will be with them and be their God." – Revelation 21:3 NIV

Since the Garden of Eden, God has longed to dwell among His people.

- In the tabernacle—His presence was among them, but distant.
- In the temple—His presence was veiled behind a curtain.

- In Jesus—His presence walked among them but was not yet fully realized.
- In the Holy Spirit—His presence now dwells within believers, but we still live in a fallen world.

But in eternity, God's presence will be fully, permanently, and intimately dwelling among us.

"They will see His face, and His name will be on their foreheads." –
Revelation 22:4 NKJV

This is the greatest joy of eternity—not just living in a beautiful city, but being with Jesus, face to face, forever.

No More Separation, No More Pain

John continues his vision with a stunning declaration:

"He will wipe every tear from their eyes. There will be no more
death, or mourning, or crying, or pain, for the former things have
passed away." – Revelation 21:4 NIV

For the Bride, this means:

- No more suffering—our earthly struggles are over.
- No more distance—we will live in constant intimacy with Jesus.
- No more longing—our hearts will be fully satisfied in His presence.

The Bride is home. The Bridegroom is with her. This is what we were created for—to dwell with Jesus in perfect, unbroken love for eternity.

3. Living as the Bride in Eternity

What Will We Do in the New Jerusalem?

Many people mistakenly think that eternity is just sitting on clouds, playing harps—but Scripture reveals something far greater.

1. We Will Reign with Christ

- "They will reign forever and ever." (Revelation 22:5)
- The Bride is not just loved—she is entrusted with authority.
- We will rule alongside Jesus, governing His eternal Kingdom.

2. We Will Worship and Minister Before Him

- "His servants will serve Him." (Revelation 22:3)
- The Bride's greatest joy will be ministering to the Bridegroom in love.
- Worship will no longer be hindered by weakness, distraction, or sin—it will be pure and perfect forever.

3. We Will Explore the Infinite Glory of God

- "The Lamb is its light." (Revelation 21:23)
- Eternity is not static—we will spend forever discovering new dimensions of God's love and glory.
- There will never be a moment of boredom, only increasing awe and wonder.

The Bride's Eternal Joy

The final vision of Scripture is not of a temple, a throne, or a battlefield—it is of a wedding and a home. The longing of the Bride is fulfilled. The waiting is over. The union is complete. This is our eternal destiny—to live as the chosen, beloved Bride of Christ.

Conclusion: The Invitation to Eternity

The final chapter of Scripture leaves us with an invitation.

"The Spirit and the Bride say, 'Come!' And let the one who hears say, 'Come!'" – Revelation 22:17 ESV

This is the cry of the mature Bride:

- She is not afraid of eternity—she longs for it.
- She is not distracted by this world—she is preparing for the next.
- She is not asleep—she is watching and waiting for her Bridegroom.

The Spirit is calling. The Bride must answer. Will we prepare for the New Jerusalem? Will we long for the return of Jesus? Will we live today as those who know eternity is near? The wedding is prepared. The King is coming. Will we be found ready?

THE CRY OF THE BRIDE AND THE SPIRIT

Introduction: The Final Cry of the Bride

Throughout history, God has been writing a divine love story — one of pursuit, redemption, preparation, and ultimate union. From the Garden of Eden to the Cross, from Pentecost to the final moments of human history, the story of the Bride and the Bridegroom has been unfolding. But the story does not end with a battle, a throne, or even the establishment of a Kingdom. It ends with a wedding and an eternal dwelling place with God. And at the very conclusion of Scripture, we hear the final words of the Bride:

"The Spirit and the Bride say, 'Come!' And let the one who hears say, 'Come!'" – Revelation 22:17 ESV

This is the ultimate prayer of love and longing—the Bride, fully awakened, crying out for her Bridegroom to return.

In this chapter, we will explore:

1. Revelation 22:17—The ultimate prayer: "Come, Lord Jesus!"
2. How the bridal paradigm fuels revival and intimacy.
3. Living daily as the Beloved of Christ.

This is the call of our generation—to live as those who are watching, waiting, and longing for the return of the Bridegroom.

1. Revelation 22:17—The Ultimate Prayer: "Come, Lord Jesus!"

The Spirit and the Bride in Agreement

At the very end of the Bible, we see a powerful moment of unity—for the first time in Scripture, the Bride is fully aligned with the Holy Spirit in intercession. "The Spirit and the Bride say, 'Come!'" This means:

- The Bride has reached full maturity, understanding her purpose and longing for Jesus.
- The Holy Spirit's deepest desire is for the return of the Bridegroom.
- The cry for Jesus' return is not just a doctrinal belief —it is the heartbeat of the Bride.

Many believers do not long for Jesus' return because they are more attached to this world than to the next. But as the Bride matures in love, her heart begins to cry out, "Come, Lord Jesus!"

"He who testifies to these things says, 'Yes, I am coming soon.' Amen. Come, Lord Jesus!" – Revelation 22:20 NIV

This is the final recorded prayer of Scripture—the last desire expressed before eternity begins. Why Does the Bride Cry, "Come"?

1. She longs for full union with the Bridegroom.

- Just as an engaged bride longs for her wedding day, the Church longs for the day of perfect union.

2. She desires justice, restoration, and the reign of Christ.

- The world is groaning for redemption (Romans 8:22).
- Only the return of the King will bring perfect righteousness and peace.

3. She is burning with love that cannot be contained.

- True love does not delay—when love is fully awakened, it cannot help but cry for the Lover's return.

The greatest tragedy would be for a Church that does not desire Jesus' coming. The greatest victory is a Bride who is fully prepared and longing for the day of union.

2. How the Bridal Paradigm Fuels Revival and Intimacy

The Cry of the Bride Ignites Revival

Wherever the Bridal Paradigm is embraced, revival follows. Why?

- When the Church sees herself as a Bride rather than just an army, worship becomes intimate, passionate, and love- driven.
- When believers understand they are loved, not just servants, prayer moves from duty to devotion.

- When the Bride longs for the Bridegroom, evangelism becomes an urgent invitation to the wedding feast.

Throughout history, great revivals have been fueled by bridal love:

- The Moravians—They lived with the motto, "That the Lamb may receive the reward of His suffering."
- The Great Awakening—Jonathan Edwards described the Church as a Bride being prepared for divine union.
- The Azusa Street Revival—Worship was marked by hunger for deeper intimacy with God.

Revival is not just about power—it is about love being fully awakened.

The Bridal Paradigm Transforms Intimacy with Jesus

When believers embrace the truth that Jesus is the Bridegroom, it changes how we approach God.

- Instead of striving for acceptance, we rest in love.
- Instead of fear-based obedience, we pursue Him out of delight.
- Instead of viewing prayer as a duty, it becomes a conversation of intimacy.

This is what Jesus desires—not just obedience, but a lovesick Bride who longs for Him.

"You shall love the Lord your God with all your heart, with all your soul, and with all your mind." – Matthew 22:37 NKJV

This is the first and greatest commandment—a call to love, not just serve.

3. Living Daily as the Beloved of Christ

What Does It Mean to Live as the Bride?

If we truly believe that:

- Jesus is returning for a Bride, not just servants...
- We are already betrothed to Him...
- Our life is preparation for a wedding day...

Then how should we live daily in light of this truth?

1. Live with First-Love Passion

- Return to a heart that burns for Jesus (Revelation 2:4-5).
- Guard against lukewarmness and distraction.
- Cultivate a lifestyle of intimacy through prayer and worship.

2. Walk in Purity and Holiness

- The Bride must make herself ready (Revelation 19:7).
- Holiness is not legalism—it is a Bride preparing for her wedding day.
- Reject anything that competes with love for Jesus.

3. Long for His Return and Live Expectantly

- A true Bride watches and waits (Matthew 25:1-13).
- This world is not our home—eternity is our destination.

- Keep oil in your lamp—live every day as though the Bridegroom could come at any moment.

4. Invite Others to the Wedding Feast

- The invitation is open—the Spirit and the Bride say, "Come" (Revelation 22:17).
- Evangelism is not just about avoiding hell—it is an invitation to be part of the greatest love story in history.
- The Bride should be so radiant with love that others are drawn to Jesus through her life.

Conclusion: The Last Call Before the Wedding

At the end of history, the Bride and the Spirit are speaking the same word: "Come, Lord Jesus." This is the final call before the wedding feast begins. The invitations have been sent. The preparations are nearly complete. The King is ready. The Bride is being made ready. The wedding is near.

The only question is: Will we be found longing, watching, and prepared? The Spirit is calling. The Bride must answer. Are you ready for the wedding? Does your heart cry, "Come, Lord Jesus"? Are you living today as the Beloved of Christ? This is our final calling—to live as a Bride in love, in purity, and in expectancy. The wedding is soon. The Spirit and the Bride say, "Come." Will you join the cry?

CONCLUSION
SAYING YES TO THE BRIDEGROOM

The Greatest Invitation in History

From the beginning of time, God has been calling a Bride for His Son. This is the story of history, the reason for creation, and the ultimate purpose of redemption—to bring forth a Bride who will love Jesus with all her heart, for all eternity. Every believer is invited into this divine romance. The question is: Will we say yes?

Saying yes to the Bridegroom is not just about salvation—it is about intimacy, transformation, and preparation. It is about moving from mere belief to burning love. At the end of all things, there will be a wedding. The Spirit and the Bride say, "Come." This final moment in history is not just an event—it is an invitation.

In this conclusion, we will explore:

1. Answering the invitation to intimacy.
2. Living in the bridal identity.
3. The coming wedding feast—the hope that sustains the Bride.

This is the greatest decision of our lives—to say yes to Jesus not just as Savior and King, but as Bridegroom.

1. Answering the Invitation to Intimacy

A Call Beyond Religion—Into Love

Many believers settle for religion when they are called to romance.

- They serve Jesus but do not love Him deeply.
- They know about Him but do not walk in intimacy.
- They wait for heaven but do not long for Him.

But the Bride's calling is different. Jesus does not want a people who just obey Him out of duty—He wants a lovesick Bride who longs for Him with all her heart. This is the difference between religion and romance:

Religion	Romance (Bridal Intimacy)
Follows rules	Follows love
Obeys out of fear	Obeys out of devotion
Performs for approval	Rests in love
Sees Jesus as King and Judge	Sees Jesus as bridegroom and lover

Jesus is calling us beyond duty into desire—beyond performance into passion. He is saying:

"Rise up, my love, my fair one, and come away." – Song of Solomon 2:10 NKJV

The question is: Will we answer?

2. Living in the Bridal Identity

Becoming the Bride He Desires

Saying yes to the Bridegroom means embracing our identity as the Bride.

- A Bride is confident in love – She knows she is chosen, loved, and pursued.
- A Bride prepares for the wedding – She keeps her lamp full of oil and her heart burning.
- A Bride longs for her Bridegroom – She watches and waits with expectancy.

Too many believers live as servants when they are called to be Brides. They see themselves as workers in the Kingdom but never as lovers in the bridal chamber. Jesus is returning for a radiant, prepared Bride—not one who is hesitant or distracted. Paul reminds us of this high calling:

"I have betrothed you to one husband, that I may present you as a chaste virgin to Christ." – 2 Corinthians 11:2 NKJV

This is our true identity. This is who we were created to be. The moment we fully embrace this reality, everything changes:

- Worship becomes love songs to the King.
- Prayer becomes intimate communion with the Bridegroom.
- Holiness becomes preparation for the wedding day.

We no longer live for this world—we live for eternal union with Jesus. The Bride is waking up to her destiny.

3. The Coming Wedding Feast—The Hope That Sustains the Bride

Living with Eyes on Eternity

Jesus spoke of a great wedding feast that would take place at the end of the age:

"Blessed are those who are invited to the wedding supper of the Lamb!" – Revelation 19:9 NIV

This wedding is not a metaphor—it is real.

- There is a table being prepared.
- There are seats reserved for the faithful.
- There is a moment coming when the waiting will be over, and the Bride will finally be with the Bridegroom.

This is the great hope that sustains the Bride—the reality that we will see Him, face to face, forever. Paul wrote of this glorious moment:

"For now we see in a mirror, dimly, but then face to face. Now I know in part, but then I shall know fully, even as I am fully known." – 1 Corinthians 13:12 NKJV

On that day:

- Every tear will be wiped away (Revelation 21:4).
- Every pain will be forgotten.
- Every longing will be satisfied.

This is what we live for. This is why we say yes to the Bridegroom now—because we are preparing for the greatest moment in history.

Conclusion: Will You Say Yes?

At the end of time, there will only be two types of people:

1. Those who are ready for the wedding.
2. Those who are not.

The invitations have been sent. The preparations are nearly complete. The wedding is coming. The Bridegroom is at the door. The Spirit is calling. The Bride must answer. Will you live as the Beloved of Christ? Will you embrace your identity as the Bride? Will your heart cry, "Come, Lord Jesus" with passion and longing? The King is ready. The feast is prepared. The door is about to open. The only question left is: Will you be found ready?

Final Prayer of Consecration

If you desire to fully embrace your bridal identity, pray this prayer:

Jesus, my Bridegroom, I say yes to You. I surrender my heart, my love, and my life to You. I choose to prepare myself as Your Bride, to walk in purity and devotion. Let my heart burn with longing for You. Let my life reflect my love for You. I join the Spirit in saying, "Come, Lord Jesus." Make me ready for the wedding feast. I am Yours forever. Amen.

APPENDIX A
STUDY GUIDE QUESTIONS FOR PERSONAL REFLECTION OR GROUP DISCUSSION

These questions are designed to help individuals or groups reflect on the Bridal Paradigm and deepen their relationship with Jesus as the Bridegroom.

Chapter 1: The King's Unfathomable Love

1. How does seeing the Song of Solomon as an allegory for Christ and the Church change your understanding of God's love?
2. Have you ever felt unworthy of God's love? How does the truth that He chooses and pursues you change that perception?
3. In what ways has Jesus wooed your heart throughout your spiritual journey?

Chapter 2: The Bride's Insecurity and the King's Assurance

1. Why do you think the Bride in Song of Solomon struggles with feelings of unworthiness ("I am dark but lovely")?
2. How can you personally relate to the tension between feeling unworthy and yet chosen?
3. What are practical ways you can start seeing yourself through the King's eyes rather than your own insecurities?

Chapter 3: The Wilderness of Love

1. Have you ever gone through a season where God felt distant? How did it shape your faith?
2. What does it mean to seek Jesus in the night seasons of your life (Song of Solomon 3:1-3)?
3. Why does God sometimes lead us into seasons of testing before deeper intimacy?

Chapter 4: The Bridal Identity

1. What does it mean to belong to Jesus ("I am my Beloved's, and He is mine" - Song of Solomon 6:3)?
2. How does embracing your Bridal Identity change the way you approach worship, prayer, and obedience?

3. In what ways is God transforming you from a servant into a bride?

Chapter 5: God as Husband in the Old Testament

1. How does seeing Israel as God's Bride change your understanding of the Old Testament?
2. What lessons can we learn from Hosea's relentless love for Gomer about God's faithfulness?
3. How do you see God pursuing and calling you back to intimacy today?

Chapter 6: Jesus as the Bridegroom in the New Testament

1. Why does John the Baptist call Jesus the Bridegroom (John 3:29)?
2. How does the Wedding at Cana foreshadow the ultimate marriage between Christ and the Church?
3. In Jesus' parables, who is invited to the wedding feast? What does this mean for us?

Chapter 7: The Ten Virgins—The Bridesmaids in the Kingdom

1. What is the significance of the oil in the parable of the Ten Virgins (Matthew 25:1-13)?
2. How can we store up oil in our spiritual lives?
3. What does this parable teach about being prepared for the return of the Bridegroom?

Chapter 8: The Apostolic Revelation of the Bride

1. Paul calls marriage a great mystery that points to Christ and the Church (Ephesians 5:32). How does this impact your view of marriage and the Church?
2. What does it mean to be betrothed to Christ (2 Corinthians 11:2)?
3. How does the cry "Come, Lord Jesus" (Revelation 22:17) reveal the heart of the Bride?

Chapter 9: The Wedding in Heaven

1. What does the Marriage Supper of the Lamb represent? (Revelation 19:7-9)
2. What is the bridal garment we will wear, and how do we prepare for it?

3. What emotions stir in your heart when you think of the moment Jesus takes His Bride home?

Chapter 10: The New Jerusalem—The Bride Prepared

1. How does the New Jerusalem as the Bride challenge traditional ideas of heaven (Revelation 21:2-3)?
2. What does it mean that God will dwell with His people forever?
3. How does knowing your eternal destiny as the Bride impact your daily life now?

Chapter 11: The Cry of the Bride and the Spirit

1. How does the cry "Come, Lord Jesus" become a reality in your life?
2. What role does intimacy with Jesus play in preparing for revival?
3. How can you live daily as the Beloved of Christ?

APPENDIX B
A PRAYER OF CONSECRATION FOR EMBRACING THE BRIDAL IDENTITY

Jesus, my Bridegroom, I come before You with an open heart. Today, I choose to embrace my identity as Your Bride—fully loved, fully chosen, and fully Yours. I lay down every insecurity, every fear, and every doubt, and I receive the garment of righteousness You have given me. I say yes to intimacy with You. I say yes to preparing my heart for Your return. I say yes to being a Bride who is watching, waiting, and longing for You. Fill my heart with fresh oil—the oil of intimacy, passion, and devotion. Let me be like the wise virgins, ready and burning with love. I surrender everything to You, Jesus. Consume me with Your love, and awaken my heart to long for You above all else. Come, Lord Jesus! I am Yours forever. Amen.

APPENDIX C

A CHART OF BRIDAL IMAGERY IN SCRIPTURE

Theme	Old Testament Shadow	New Testament Fulfillment
God as Husband	"Your Maker is your husband" (Isaiah 54:5)	"Christ loved the Church and gave Himself up for her" (Ephesians 5:25)
Israel as the Bride	God betrothed Israel to Himself but she was unfaithful (Hosea 2:19-20)	The Church is betrothed to Christ (2 Corinthians 11:2)
The Betrothal Process	A Jewish bride was legally betrothed but waited for her groom	We are engaged to Christ but waiting for the wedding (John 14:2-3)
The Wedding Feast	God's covenants with Israel foreshadowed a great banquet	The Marriage Supper of the Lamb (Revelation 19:7-9)
The Bride's Preparation	Esther went through a year of purification before meeting the king (Esther 2:12)	The Church is being made ready, clothed in righteousness (Revelation 19:8)
The Bridegroom's Return	Jewish grooms came unexpectedly at night for their brides	Jesus will come like a thief in the night (Matthew 25:1-13)
The Cry of the Bride	The psalmist longs for God's presence (Psalm 42:1)	The Bride and the Spirit cry, "Come, Lord Jesus!" (Revelation 22:17)

Final Thought: The bridal paradigm is not just a theological concept—it is an invitation into the greatest love story of all time. The Bridegroom is calling. The wedding is being prepared. The Spirit is stirring the hearts of the Bride. Will we say yes?

ABOUT THE AUTHOR

Tom Cornell is the Senior Leader of SOZO Church in Washington state, founder of Walk in the Light International and SOZO Network. Tom is married to his beautiful wife Katy and lives in the Puget Sound area with her and their three kids. He has been in ministry pastoring and teaching the body of Christ since 2008.

He has a passion to see the body of Christ moving from people with an orphan mindset to that of sonship; equipping the body to do the work of Jesus resulting in seeing the Kingdom of God manifested here on earth.